THIS IS BASEBALL

by **Margaret Blackstone**
pictures by **John O'Brien**

Henry Holt and Company ◆ New York

For my father, Henry
my son, Dash
my husband, Tom
and my brothers, Pete and Neil
all great boys of summer
and for my friend, Elissa
one of the great girls of all seasons
—M.B.

For Tessie,
the first in my lineup
—J.O'B.

Henry Holt and Company, LLC, *Publishers since 1866,* 175 Fifth Avenue, New York, New York 10010
mackids.com

Library of Congress Cataloging-in-Publication Data
Blackstone, Margaret / This is baseball / by Margaret Blackstone; pictures by John O'Brien.
Summary: A simple introduction to the game of baseball, covering its equipment, players, and basic plays.
The illustrations show a game in progress.   1. Baseball—Juvenile literature.   {1. Baseball.}
I. O'Brien, John, ill.   II. Title.   GV867.5.B57   1993   796.357—dc20   92-22921

ISBN 978-0-8050-5169-8
First published in hardcover in 1993 by Henry Holt and Company
First paperback edition—1997
Printed in China by South China Printing Company Ltd.,
Dongguan City, Guangdong Province
16   18   20   19   17   15

THIS IS BASEBALL

This is a stadium,

and this is a baseball diamond.

This is one team,

and this is the other.

These are the fans.

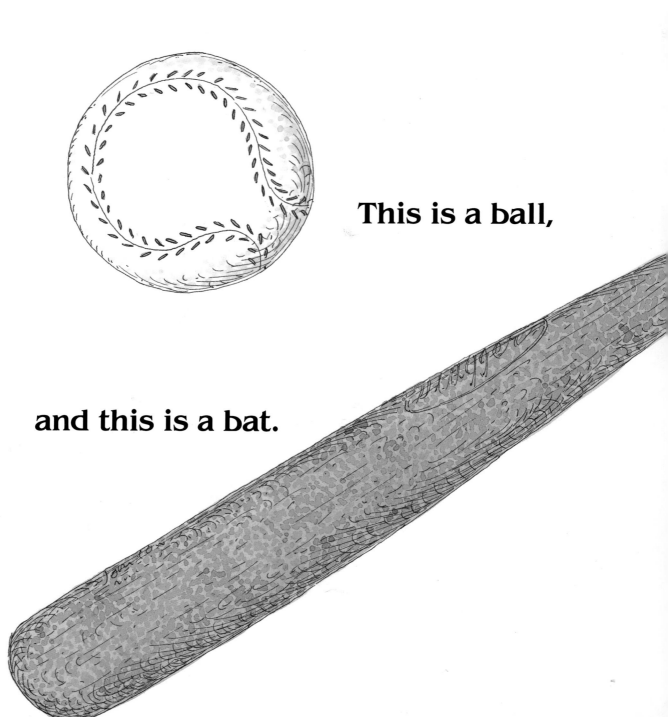

This is a ball,

and this is a bat.

This is a glove,

and this is a cap.

This is a player.

And these are the umpires who call the game.

This is a pitcher.

This is a catcher.

This is the infield.

This is the outfield.

This is a pitch.

And this is a hit!

This is a high fly ball to deep left field...

and this is a
HOME RUN!

This team has won,

and this team has lost.

Tomorrow there will be another game.